Advanced Reading & Writing Skills

- **Editing**
- **Fluency**
- **You're the Editor**
- **Writing an Informational Paragraph**
- **Presuasive Writing Techniques**

On Board
ACADEMICS

Advanced Reading and Writing Skills

© 2015 OnBoard Academics, Inc
Portsmouth, NH
800-596-3175
www.onboardacademics.com
ISBN: 978-1-63096-040-7

OnBoard Academic's books are specifically designed to be used as printed workbooks or as on-screen instruction. Each page offers focused exercises and students quickly master topics with enough proficiency to move on to the next level.

OnBoard Academic's lessons are used in over 25,000 classrooms to rave reviews. Our lessons are aligned to the most recent governmental standards and are updated from time to time as standards change. Correlation documents are located on our website. Our lessons are created, edited and evaluated by educators to ensure top quality and real life success.

Interactive lessons for digital whiteboards, mobile devices, and PCs are available at www.onboardacademics.com. These interactive lessons make great additions to our books.

You can always reach us at customerservice@onboardacademics.com.

Editing

Key Vocabulary

editing

Editing

> **Editing** is when you check for correct **capitalization**, **punctuation** and **spelling**.

Do you notice any mistakes?

i have to do my homework tonight.

Lets get some vanilla ice cream!

The porcipine is very prickly.

Here are the edited sentences.

I *correct capitalization*

have to do my homework tonight.

Let's *correct punctuation*

get some vanilla ice cream!

porcupine *correct spelling*

The porcipine **is very prickly.**

Edit Capitalization

When editing text, remember that every sentence begins with a capital letter, and the word I and names are always capitalized.

Edit the following sentences.

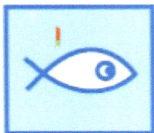

we are taking a trip to the aquarium.

i was waiting outside with my classmates.

the bus was running late to pick us up.

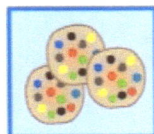

Everyone was glad owen brought cookies.

Edit Punctuation

When editing text for punctuation, remember that every sentence ends with a **punctuation mark**, a **comma** is used to insert a pause, and an **apostrophe** is used to make a contraction.

Edit the following sentences.

I bought new shoes today

What color did you buy

I bought red and white sneakers

I cant wait to play basketball in them

.   ,   ?   !   '

Edit the spelling.

Running is a good way to exersise.

You can run in youree neighborhood.

It's fun to be ouetsde in the fresh air!

Wheree do you like to run?

Which sentences need editing. Mark each sentence with the key below.

C	capitalization error
P	punctuation error
S	spelling error
✓	sentence is OK

	Alisons Dad drove her to the park.
C	I like games music and baseball.
P	when did you get here?
S	The leaves crunched underfoot.
✓	Will you read me a story?
	The backpak was really heavy.

Edit the story.

"The Last Slice of Cake"
By: Tori Garcia

Its a lazy afternoon in the town of Shelton

Everyone is relaxing and siping lemonade.

everyone except Brian; hes racing across

the open field charging over branchs and

smalle brooks. brian needs to get home

before his sister takes the last slic of cake

Look at the next page for the answer.

Here is the story edited.
Did you find all of the mistakes?

"The Last Slice of Cake"
By: Tori Garcia

It's a lazy afternoon in the town of Shelton

Everyone is relaxing and sipping lemonade.

Everyone except Brian; he's racing across

the open field charging over branches and

small brooks. Brian needs to get home

before his sister takes the last slice of cake.

Name_____

Editing Quiz

1. You only need to check for spelling when editing text. True or false?

2. Circle the sentence that has been edited correctly?
   a. The sky is a deep blue color.
   b. the sky is a deep blue color.
   c. The sky is a deep blue color
   d. The sky is a deap blue color.

3. Edit the sentence. I love thunderstorms

4. Edit this sentence. Sharon and i are on the phone.

5. What needs to be edited in this sentence. Circle one. Where is my backpack
   a. Capitalization
   b. Punctuation
   c. Spelling
   d. None of the above
   e.
   f.

6. What needs to be edited in this sentence. Circle one. It's so nice to see you!
   a. Capitalization
   b. Punctuation
   c. Spelling
   d. None of the above

Fluency

Key Vocabulary

fluency

speed

accuracy

intonation

context

Fluency is the ability to read text with the proper speed, accuracy and intonation.

Roses are red
Violets are blue
Sugar is sweet
And, so are you

Read the poem three different ways.
Put a check in the circle when you achieved description below. If possible read to another person and ask them if you achieved the description

| slow and impassive | normal and fluent | fast and hard to understand |

Does the conversation fit with
the context and the punctuation?

"Do you see what I see?"

"It's snowing outside!"

"Let's make a snowman."

Would it be correct to read the above passage in a very slow and boring fashion? Try it and see.

Context and Punctuation

A good pace sounds like natural conversation, a nd the correct intonation would help us to understand that the boys are excited...Look for clues in **context and punctuation.**

www.onboardacademics.com

Punctuation and Fluency

> **Punctuation marks** indicate how a sentence should be read.

Read the sentence and use the punctuation in red as a clue to the way it should be read.

"How was your soccer game, Owen?"

"It was great, Mom! I scored a goal!"

"The coach seemed really happy."

Use context and punctuation clues to fill in the missing words.

Action verbs such as *shouted*, *roared*, and *whispered* give clues to the intonation of a sentence.

"Don't run with scissors!" his mother [   ].

The airplane engines [   ] into life.

"The baby is sleeping," the boy [   ].

roared	whispered	shouted

    www.onboardacademics.com

Name_____

Fluency Quiz

1. Fluency is the ability to read text with proper speed, accuracy and intonation. True or false?

2. Action verbs give clues to the intonation of a sentence. True or false?

3. Punctuation marks are not helpful to someone reading a story. True or false?

You're the Editor

Key Vocabulary

revise

edit

Edit

Edit this student's essay.

> To **edit** means to correct errors, such as spelling or punctuation. This is different than revising, which means to make changes to the structure or the content of a text.

We went to to vermont a vacation. My unclle has a Cabin there and he let us use it.

Stay as long as you want, he said

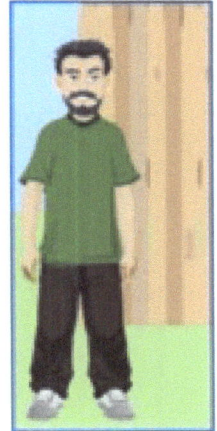

> How could you communicate more clearly to the student the changes that are needed?

Edit Symbols

Label each edit instruction with the proper symbol.

We went to t̸o vermont *for* a vacation. My ⟨unclle⟩ *uncle* has a Çabin there, and he let us use it.

"Stay as long as you want, he said ⊙

	spelling error			insert quote marks
	delete			insert comma
	capitalize letter			insert period
	lowercase letter			insert something

⊙   ∧   ≡   /   sp.   ∧   ˅˅   ℯℓ

     www.onboardacademics.com

Edit with Symbols

Edit these texts using the symbols provided.

My Teacher explayned that when editing text you should always look carefuly for spelling and punctuation, grammatical errors

He said, "the difference between something good and something great is is attention to detail.

⊙   ∧   ≡   /   sp.   ∧̣   ̈v̈ v̈"   ℘

The Internet got started in the 1960s, when US Military developed a sieries of connected computer networks that would be able two function in a crisis. The national science foundation then applyed this idea to help build a Network that would be used be throughout the world for academic personal, and commercial purposes

          www.onboardacademics.com

Name_____

You're the Editor Quiz

1. Draw the symbol for delete. _____

2. Name the error. I live in the blue house on Main street.
   a. spelling
   b. capitalization
   c. punctuation
   d. no error

3. Name the error.
   a. spelling capitalization
   b. punctuation
   c. no errors

4. Name the error. My mom said, Happy birthday!"
   a. spelling
   b. capitalization
   c. punctuation
   d. no errors

5. Name the error? _____

6. Name the error. I bought stickers pencils and erasers for the class.
   a. spelling
   b. capitalization
   c. punctuation

Writing an Informational Paragraph

Key Vocabulary

paragraph

Topic Sentence

> **Well-written informational paragraphs often begin with a clear topic sentence. A topic sentence tells the reader up-front what the paragraph is all about.**

_____

Below is the first sentence of a paragraph. What is the paragraph about?

There are many exciting things to see and do in Boston.

_____
_____
_____
_____

Clear Topic Sentences

Order these topic sentence by how clear they are about the topic of the paragraph.

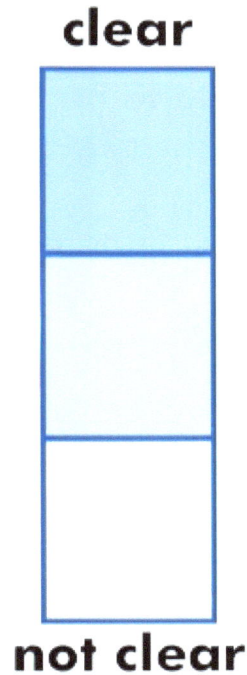

clear

A The average amount of rainfall in Seattle is about 36 inches per year.

B If you've never seen a game of rugby before, understanding a few basic rules will help you.

C When I left the house today, my mom waved goodbye from the bedroom window.

not clear

Detail Sentences

Detail sentences support topic sentences, providing more detail or supporting information

The United Nations is an international organization that was founded after World War II with the goal of helping to make the world a better and more peaceful place. Almost every country in the world is a member of the UN, and member countries send representatives to the main UN building in New York City to discuss issues and make decisions. Peacekeeping is one very high profile role of the UN, and UN peacekeepers are identified by their distinctive blue helmets.

topic sentence
detail sentence

Topic and Detail Sentences

Sort the sentence by placing the topic sentence in the blue box and the detail sentences in the white boxes.

Her supporters became known as suffragettes.

Emmeline Pankhurst fought for a woman's right to vote.

They sometimes used violence to draw attention to their cause.

―――――――――――――

She is credited with saving the life of John Smith, an early settler.

In 1614, she married an Englishman called John Rolfe.

Pocahontas was the daughter of Chief Powhatan.

―――――――――――――

As a result of this, she was arrested, fined, and lost her job.

Rosa Parks has been called the "mother" of the civil rights movement.

In 1955, she refused to give up her seat on a bus to a white man.

Wrap-up Sentences

There are a number of things you can do to keep your pets safe from coyotes. Most importantly, do not leave them unsupervised outside for long periods of time. Build a fence to keep coyotes out of your yard, and don't leave food outside since this may attract coyotes to your property. Outside cats are very vulnerable, so consider keeping your cat inside at all times. When walking a dog, keep it leashed to reduce the likelihood of a coyote encounter. If you follow these simple rules, your pet will have a good chance of avoiding joining a coyote for dinner!

Well-written informational paragraphs often end with a clear wrap-up sentence. The wrap-up, or closing sentence, often restates the topic sentence.

Comment on these alternate wrap-up sentences.

The *method of loci* is a great way to remember things. First, take a mental walk through your house. As you go, create mental notes of particular parts of the house, e.g the front door, the hallway rug, etc.. These are your *loci*. Practice until you can consistently go from loci to loci. Then, when you need to remember a list, mentally place each item in the list on a loci. For example, *Mercury* is on the door, *Venus* is on the hallway rug, *Earth* is on the mirror, etc..

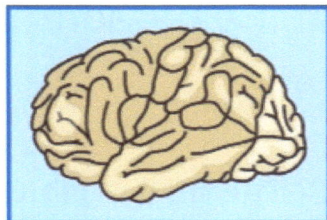

1. It doesn't have to be a list of planets, of course!
2. You'll be amazed at how good your memory actually is!
3. My memory is pretty awful!

Comments

1. _____

_____

_____

2. _____

_____

_____

3. _____

_____

_____

www.onboardacademics.com

Name_____

Writing an Informational Paragraph Quiz

1. A topic sentence clearly expresses what the paragraph will be about. True or false?

2. A wrap-up sentence restates the topic sentence. True or false?

3. Which is the clearest topic sentence?
    a. I'd like to inherit a million dollars one day.
    b. A million dollars is a lot of money.
    c. I'm not sure if I have any rich, elderly relatives.
    d. I know what I'd do if I found a million dollars.

4. Which detail sentences does not belong with this topic sentence: Steven Spielberg is a famous Hollywood director.
    a. One of his best-loved movies is ET.
    b. Many people believe that aliens do not exist.
    c. He attended film school in California.
    d. His first film was called Amblin

5. Topic sentences, detail sentences and wrap up sentences can be in any order. True of false?

Persuasive Writing

Key Vocabulary

persuade

argument

elaboration

hook

endorsement

controversial

provocative

thesis

Key Elements of Persuasive Writing

1	**Strong opening "hook"**
2	**Evidence, elaboration, examples, including statistics or research**
3	**Acknowledge opposing point of view**
4	**Controversial or provocative statements**
5	**Appeal to emotions, e.g. hopes, fears, empathy, etc.**
6	**Endorsements or support of famous people**
7	**Conclusions which restate or summarize argument**
8	**A clear "call for action" (what should happen next)**

Can you identify the 8 key elements of persuasive writing in this passage?

I'm asking the citizens of this great city for their vote so that I can finish the job I started 4 years ago! During my first term in office, spending on education has risen by 300%, crime is down 4%, and we've reduced the budget deficit. While it's true that we were forced to raise taxes, my opponent in this race plans to save money by slashing vital programs like the fuel allowance for the elderly! That's why I've been endorsed by the Pensioners Action Group. So, if you want better schools, lower crime, and support for the elderly, then vote for me... and let's finished what we started!

Summarizing Arguments.

Fernando thinks it's ok to watch and download movies from illegal websites. Mia thinks it's wrong. Summarize their arguments and say which one you find more persuasive.

> I think its ok to watch boot leg movies on the web. I read somewhere that 95% of all viewed movies on the internet are viewed for free illegally. Most other things on the web are free so movies should be free too. Also, I only get a small allowance so I can't afford to pay for movies.

■ _____

■ _____

_____ ■ _____

_____

> Lets call watching boot leg movies what it is; theft. You wouldn't defend stealing something from a store but think its ok to illegally watch movies. Its morally wrong. Whey you download movies from illegal sites you are exposing your computer to viruses and other security threats. You are

■ _____

■ _____

_____ ■ _____

Argument Strength.

> The principal has announced that cell phones will be banned on all school premises. Rate each of these arguments against the ban in terms of how persuasive they are. 5 means very persuasive. 0 means not persuasive at all.

Rank

1 It's just not fair!

2 Students will find a way to get around the ban.

3 The current rules for cell phones are working fine.

4 Cell phones can be an important educational tool.

5 Studies have shown they distract students.

6 Students need phones to stay in touch with parents.

> This is an open-ended question, so there are no "right" answers. However, argument 1 isn't very persuasive, and argument 5 is an argument *in favor* of a ban.

Persuasive or Not?

> **"I think the school week should be reduced to 4 days."**

Consider the thesis above and decide which three arguments or elaborations might be persuasive if you were concerned about the effect of a shorter week on student attainment?

1	
2	
3	

This would increase motivation and reduce burn out.

I don't think student attainment would suffer.

It would save the town money on salaries and utilities.

The length of the school day could be increased.

There would be no need for a long summer vacation.

Students could focus more time on their hobbies.

Topic and Author's Purpose

Based on the following persuasive points can you figure out what is the topic and what is the author's purpose?

> **Topic** means the general subject matter, and **author's purpose** means the author's main reason for writing.

■ It causes more than 440,000 deaths each year.

■ It makes your clothes and your hair smell bad.

■ It's harmful to your friends and family members.

■ It makes your skin look old and wrinkly.

■ It's illegal in most states until you're 18.

Topic: _____

_____

_____

Author's Purpose: _____

Hook and Wrap

Write a strong first "hook" and a lat sentence "wrap for this anti-smoking passage.

_____

_____

Well, you may not be aware that smoking causes more than 440,000 deaths each year in the US. Definitely not cool. And you're not just harming yourself either. Secondhand smoke is harmful to your friends and family, causing an estimated 50,000 deaths each year. Smoking makes your clothes and your hair smell bad as well, and it will make your skin look old and wrinkly. How cool is that? And by the way, it's also illegal to smoke until you're at least 18 in most most states.

_____

_____

Name_____

Persuasive Writing Quiz

1. A call to action in persuasive writing means what the author wants you to do next. True or false?

2. Appealing to emotions is a key element of persuasive writing. True or false?

3. Writers should include a "hook" at the end of persuasive writing. True or false?

4. If one argument is "This would help to increase student attainment"' what is the least likely thesis?
   a. We should end the long summer vacation.
   b. Every student should have a laptop.
   c. School sports help to improve health
   d. We should reduce class sizes by 25%

5. Which argument does not support the thesis that students should go to school seven days per week?
   a. Students will be more prepared for careers.
   b. Five days is not enough to cover learning material
   c. Students need time to rest.
   d. Schools could offer an extended vacation.

www.ingramcontent.com/pod-product-compliance
Lightning Source LLC
Chambersburg PA
CBHW060815090426
42737CB00002B/72